Thank you for your support !
609-892-6543
Anointed scribe

Identity Deception
From Wounds to Worship

Evangelist
Tamika Strickland

DEDICATION

I dedicate this book to my Lord and Savior Jesus Christ aka "Daddy". I thank you for all that I have gone through, walked through, and healed through. You have given me a second chance at life, and I am grateful to you. The revelation and knowledge that you give me as my hunger and love for you grows, is like a burning light that gives me strength. It keeps me searching for more wisdom. I love you Father God.

~

Mom, I remember you asking auntie, "when is she going to be happy?" I was angry about that, but truth be told you were right. I met Jesus Mommy and He changed the condition of my heart one day at a time. I dedicate this book to you Mommy, and I thank you for loving me unconditionally. I know that when this book is truly launched, you will be shining your light on me that day. We love and miss you so much.

TABLE OF CONTENTS

ACKNOWLEDGMENTS

I would like to thank all my family and friends who supported me through this faith walk with God. To my auntie, Carol Ford, what a brilliant woman you are. You gave me strength and wisdom like only you can. LOVE U AUNTIE.

To Apostle Robbin Hargrove, my shepherd, thank you for all that you have done in my life. I'm grateful for you and the Women of Deliverance. That night was the beginning of my destiny with God. Thank you, and I love you.

Thank you, Elder-Elect Sabrina Showell (DEEP, LLC) for taking this walk with me and God. You are an inspiration to us all in the anointed scribe world.

I thank everyone who has been a part of my life and transformation. You know who you are. I love u family and friends.

FOREWORD

The biblical reference of **Restoration** has begun to push into the **Season of Birthing**! The days of being *stuck* are over! The Lord wants His People to be free and whole. The book**, _Identity Deception: From Wounds to Worship_** is a powerful, illuminating, thought provoking transformational description of how God, when we allow Him, can bring us through any storm; delivered and restored!

I am an uncle to the author. I was present when she was born and have when the occasion presented itself, ministered to her with prayer and direct contact, been part of her life. In the past thirty years I have been involved in ministry in one way or another. I am now serving humanity as Sr. Pastor of the Shepherd's House of Restoration Worship Center, Inc., located in Maryland. My wife and I co-pastor a *Ministry of Restoration* that has allowed me to delve deeply into all aspects of restoration that involve victims of all types of abuse.

Identity Deception: From Wounds to Worship is a MUST READ for everybody. The author candidly *opens up* her life to the reader by sharing places of intimate struggles as a result of sexual abuse early in her life; which altered the course of her life. The author, by being transparent, skillfully guides the reader through each phase of her life journey, highlighting the pain associated with the aftermath of abuse. The reader will crave for more as the story unfolds right before their eyes.

Two issues will emerge as the author chronicles her experiences. The first issue is predicated on how strong the *spirits of abandonment and rejection* are and their ability to keep you bound up: mind, body and spirit. The second issue that surfaces is whether God's love is strong enough to bring you out of the trials and struggles associated with coming to terms with the abuse. In her pursuit of love, she turns to a lifestyle of seeking *Eros love* from other women. The story will intensify as the author shares how she obtained the ultimate victory of *Agape love,* by turning completely to God. One interpretation of agape love states, "Agape love is not friend, sexual, or brotherly love, but it's sacrificial love. It shows action. When we are always worried about *self,* we will never have this type of love. God's agape love is in believers. "Do all things with the love of God expecting nothing in return" (Biblereasons.com).

This book is *drama packed* and will surely answer many questions that persons may have in similar circumstances. I believe that this book just scratches the surface; opening up a dialogue of true restoration and healing for all victims of abuse. No Time Like the Present! Turn the pages and prepare to feel the author's pain; journey through looking for love in unexpected places; a Divine encounter with God; and eyes wide open; healing and restoring **from wounds to worship!**

Written by
Bishop Randolph O. Perry, PhD, EdD,
Senior Pastor, Shepherds' House of Restoration
(SHR), Clinton, MD, 2019

INTRODUCTION

When you don't know who you are in Christ Jesus, your life will be unfulfilled. Knowing your purpose and value will bring you inner joy, a healthy state of mind, and give you strength. I have allowed other people's words and actions mold me into someone I was unhappy with. I was insecure and it distorted my body image and led me down a path of illusion and self-destruction. I was constantly searching for someone or something to fill the voids. It was like a toothache that repeatedly reminded me that I was in need of healing, but I accepted the wrong outlets for healing. I fell in love with women, thinking being a lesbian would make me whole. I was unable to truly feel their love, unless it was sexually, but after a while, that didn't sustain me.

The aching grew worse and I became desperate, getting lost in a world of drugs and painful relationships. I thought I could never get out of that life. I was never content with myself, always seeking and wishing for change. I blamed others for my life and how I felt. Even if someone offered me joyous moments, my hurt destroyed the relationship as I took them as my emotional hostage.

I have learned that people dress up and wear masks to hide their internal wounds. People would never think that I was broken by looking at my pretty face. The pain I felt from a young age cultivated a life of insecurity. Insecurity further damaged me as I damaged others. The void I felt from the damage could no longer be contained, so I tried to cover it. I covered up so much that I had no idea who I was. I believed what others told me, but it was all lies and deception.

I met God after many failed attempts. Fear kept me running from Him, but deep desperation kept me walking towards him. I wanted to end a vicious cycle, an endless loop of depression and pain so I stopped running from God. I realized later in life that if God isn't in it, then nothing positive would ever come out of it. I stopped participating in behaviors that hindered my walk with Christ. I didn't know how I was going to be relieved, but I was willing to take a chance with Him. I followed His guidelines and developed a hunger to know Him more and more. I lost my desire to be with anyone that was blocking me from God and that meant leaving my lesbian lifestyle behind. As I began my true walk with God, it seemed as if my life was falling apart.

God is always speaking. Each time that sin was involved, His voice would become distant and it eventually felt like I was on my own. With His help I opened my spiritual eyes and saw that God gave me a gift of life. God gives us free will so He will never force His love upon anyone, we must surrender. The key is remaining teachable, while God, the teacher teaches. Let me show you how I finally surrendered to God's will.

John 8:36
"If the son therefore shall make you free,
ye shall be free indeed."

Chapter 1
LITTLE TAMIKA

Let's gather around the dinner table. Go back to your childhood and remember what it was like to eat with your family. My dinner table was nothing like some modern Jewish families. Why? Well, there's an awesome tradition in which Jewish fathers bless their children while eating together. The children anticipate their daily blessing and much respect is given to these fathers – but that's another subject for another time. The American culture used to somewhat adopt this by having the entire family gather at the table, share their day to day activities, and the fathers would offer his thoughts. The difference is that when Jewish fathers bless their children, they say great things about them.

Can you imagine sitting around your dinner table and

your father telling you how great you are? Some of us didn't grow up with a father, but if you did, could you daydream about the good things he would have said to you? Would he call you his princess, profess how much he loved you, or publicly let everyone know how special you were to him? That was my daydream – to be loved by my father and mother. Little Tamika wanted to be daddy's little girl. She wanted to be her father's princess. She wanted to be able to run to him when she was sad or angry. Little Tamika wanted a bond so strong that superman himself couldn't break it. She wanted to share her heart with her father and let him wipe her tears when she cried. She wanted to cling to him for protection and be mad when he overprotected her. In her mind, this was what true love was all about – clinging to her father, but there was one problem with Little Tamika's idea of love – how could she cling to the person that repeatedly sexually abused her? Being a daddy's girl wasn't my reality. I didn't have the beautiful memories that some little girls talk about (if you do then know that you're blessed beyond measure). Instead, I felt partial love and it kept me wanting and wishing for more. I remember being violated, being touched between my legs. I would shake because I didn't like how it felt and in my little heart, I knew it wasn't okay. When he laughed as I shook, I hated him, even if I didn't know what hate was.

Needless to say, everything I believed about love was lost at an early age. In fact, I was eight years old when I lost Little Tamika, my identity, or any sense of understanding of who I truly was. I never understood why, but as I look back, I've realized that my detrimental brokenness came from a failed relationship. When my parent's relationship ended, I began a downhill journey. Although my relationship with my father wasn't the best, the painful separation from him devastated me without my permission. I coped the best way I could, but brokenness became my way of life. It led me to deceive myself as I searched for the true love of my father in all the wrong places. The love I longed for was no longer available to me, the child who looked just like him, (something my mother frequently told me).

As I was seeking to fill the void that was eating me alive, I unconsciously held tight to the spirit of abandonment. I consider this spirit to be the root of all my problems. The spirit of abandonment isn't a person or a ghost; it's a real entity that wreaks havoc in the lives of many. When my father stepped out of his position, this spirit stepped in and negatively filled the void. It was that spirit who internally voiced the lies about why my father left me. It speaks to millions of people and tells them all the same lies. It told me that I was unloved, unwanted, unnecessary, unworthy, and ugly. It made me fearful that everyone that came into my life would leave me just like my father did. When I believed those lies, it opened up my mind and emotions to allow other spirits into my life. They became strongholds or powerful fortresses that kept others out, all the while keeping me trapped inside. I felt lost and rejected.

It may seem weird that I cried out and longed for the same person that sexually abused me, but I was just a little girl that wanted a loving father. I always wondered why he would touch me inappropriately. Didn't he know that it would change my life? Didn't he know that my reality would shift, and that I would stop loving myself? Didn't he know I'd be plagued with false feelings and false love? The trauma of being touched as a little girl caused me pain and unfortunately, I tried to ease the pain with any and everything. I wanted to stop feeling lost and I longed to be secure within myself, but nothing ever filled the deep crater that abuse created. Little Tamika no longer felt like a beautiful little girl.

Little Tamika now represents and embodies my traumatic childhood. Although I tried to just live life and suppress her pain, she continually reared her wounded heart and controlled my life with her sorrow. She was subtle in how she drew me into lesbian relationships, drugs, and self-hate. This beautiful little girl was scorned and from an early age, and she took it out on me.

Chapter 2
BORN GAY

I was born in Atlantic City, New Jersey, but left when I was ten years old. For one year, I stayed in Mays Landing, a city about half an hour from Atlantic City. When my mom got married, my stepfather moved us into a large 5-bedroom house in Winslow township (about an hour from Atlantic City). My stepfather wasn't mean, but he nicknamed me "fatty" and my sister "skinny". He never knew it was causing me trauma and I never knew how to tell him to stop. All I knew was how insecure I felt.

Back in Atlantic City, the little girl in me had faded away and I became a tomboy. I gave my all to being tough like the little boys and jumped fences with my friends. In the back of my mind, I wondered why I wanted to play football and beat up the boys. I didn't let it consume me and I soon learned how to play a variety of sports and was very athletic. I was great at football, even better than some of the boys. When I moved, I tried tennis and softball. I was good at tennis, but I loved softball. My stepfather's nickname rung like an alarm inside of me as I would run around bases. I was too fat to play, and I couldn't get it out of my mind. Truth be told, I really wasn't heavy, I was athletically built. I was 5'4 and maybe 125 lbs. There was nothing wrong with me, but I couldn't see that. Being in the locker room was too hard for me, so at 16 years old, I started taking diuretics to lose weight.

I started resenting my mom; not because she didn't tell me I had a good weight, but because she started getting high. I felt as if I had to take over her motherly duties. Being the oldest, I had three younger siblings to take care of. My stepfather was always high too! He rolled joint after joint but wouldn't hesitate to wake us up if the dishes weren't done. I always told myself I wouldn't smoke because of what he did, but later in life, I ended up smoking, sometimes with him. When he introduced my mother to cocaine, things really changed. She would steal about $1000 of my money and forge my name on financial documents like credit cards. The cops came to my job to question me about those documents and I was so embarrassed.

Being a tomboy was my cover. I didn't know it, but I had become used to being tough as a way to cope with all the negative feelings I had on the inside. I overachieved in athletics, so I didn't have to deal with or think about the negativity. The only thing I could think about was how pretty the female teachers were. I always found myself looking at them and saying, "Wow! She's so pretty!" I wanted to be next to her and it caused me to become a teacher's pet. At this point, it was pure innocence. I hadn't crossed over to lesbianism just yet, in fact, most people would say that I was still figuring out who I was. They were right, I didn't know who I was. All that had happened to me caused me to lose sight of who I would have been. All I knew is that I had to protect little Tamika from being hurt or helpless again. My Aunt Carol did help me; she was a motivator in hindsight. Even though I didn't believe her, she would always tell me I was pretty. As I got older, my innocent admiration of women turned into lustful desires. The first crush I had was on my teacher. I loved her hair and her looks. It was never anything sexual, but just a perverted admiration. I felt like I needed both my Aunt and my teacher's validation.

I began to take notice of girls more and more; things I'd never noticed about myself. I had an attraction to older women. Their beauty made me feel attractive. I watched the way they walked and how their buttocks would sway from side to side. They were so beautiful, and I wasn't. I couldn't tell that I was pretty too. I would write letters to these older women and tell them how much I loved them. I wrote to them about how I wanted them to be my lover, but nothing ever happened, and I was embarrassed. I felt fat and ugly all over again. I was screaming on the inside to announce to the world what I was feeling on the inside and who I believed I was. I was gay, at least that's what my friend told me. She had concluded that this was true because I didn't wear makeup, large earrings, or switch my hips when I walked. Regardless of why she thought I was gay, the things she and my other friends told me were feeding my inner feelings. Everything they said made me think they were right.

One day, I found out my best friend had a crush on me. We were in the car and when she held my hand,

I felt like, "Wow, she must be the one!" I really wasn't attracted to her, but I was full of emotion and just went with it. Then she introduced me to the gay clubs and took me to a place I had always wanted to go called Studio 6. They had the best dance music I had ever heard. As I walked into the club, no one could tell if I was a femme (feminine lesbian) or butch (masculine lesbian) because I didn't know how to dress; I had long hair and an athletic build. No matter what, I was a newbie and was considered fresh meat. Since no one had ever seen me before, they were all talking about me. They wanted to get to know me. As I got to know more lesbians, they told me more about myself. Someone told me I was born gay and I believed them. I had always thought it was the truth, that is, until I met Jesus Christ. Back then, I believed them because I always wondered why at a young age, I looked at women the way I did. From then on, I started to live life and play the role of being gay. I did my best to be confident even though I was scared to death.

It wasn't for a while, but once I slept with a woman, it began to feel natural. It was easy to talk with her. It was easy to let my guard down, so I felt like it was the life I was supposed to live. Then one day, I had to cut off my long hair because the hairdresser severely messed it up. While my hair was short, I met a woman who decided to change my entire look. She worked at a clothing store and had me try on men's clothes. From there, I began wearing men's clothing and established myself as a butch. In any relationship you can get hurt and I did. With each painful relationship I morphed more and more into a man. Being tough was how I coped, so I kept my hair short and started boxing to get in shape. I had to look the part, even though I didn't feel comfortable in the role. It was an expectation of my peers. All I wanted was love, so I gave people the permission to change me. I had hoped that someone would just love me, Little Tamika.

Chapter 3
CHASING LOVE

After my father departed my life, I was a lost 8-year-old who no longer trusted anyone. I was searching for a love that no human could ever give. As time moved forward, the thorn of a lost love grew larger and larger. I had to ease the pain. I had to fill the void. I had to find what I was missing and so I began chasing people and things to help remove the thorn. The chase for love consumed me. I found and believed in false love and broken relationships, but it just covered up the wound with a band-aid. The band-aid couldn't cover it for long. It began oozing out of me and it smelled like death all the time.

As a child, I didn't understand that the feelings I felt reflected the pain of my father leaving me with a desire for more than partial love. I reacted from a place of feeling abandoned or rejected. No matter the situation, these two spirits were always ready to stand up and let everyone know how truly broken I really was. I needed someone to realize that I had a thorn. I wanted someone to understand how deeply hurt I was, and I developed a habit of seeking attention at every moment. I couldn't get enough of it. When you gave me attention, I needed more. When you stopped, I felt a gut-wrenching blow of loss and rejection. I felt sick inside and I was afraid that I was nothing unless you stayed by my side to love me again. Little Tamika would come out and scream on the inside, "don't leave me like my dad did!" My mind was under attack and I believed the lies. I believed that everyone would leave me like my father did. I believed I was never good enough for someone to stay. I was always in fear and I doubted my existence and purpose in life. I searched for others to validate me – the way I looked, how I dressed, who I was. I desired their love, so that I didn't have to love myself. I thought that if you left me, I would die all over again. I had all of these feelings on the inside, but I was never physically with any woman at this point.

I didn't understand why I felt that way, but I didn't care why or where it came from either. I didn't love who I was, and I didn't like what I looked like. I was repeatedly told that I looked like my father, "the man that left". It made me angry because he left me too! So, I searched for a replacement, someone that would love me enough to remove the thorn of abandonment and abuse. I only cared that you knew how much I needed you. I only cared that you would show me love – no, that you HAD to show me love or else little Tamika would cry out.

As I entered into relationships, I would start out being that person who you felt the need to get to know on an intimate basis. I appeared confident and was adorable to look at. The package seemed like a winner, but it was all a mask. Women fell for the mask and I walked through a door that in hindsight, I never really wanted to go through. Since I was searching for a fix and these women gave me the attention that I thought I needed, I continued with the relationship. While in a relationship, I would act as if it was okay for you to have plans with other people that didn't include me, but I was honestly hurt. I realized, I was unable to truly be happy with or without you. On the inside, I was slowly feeling the loss of daddy, and that's when Little Tamika would show up.

When she arrived, she would make you feel like you were totally responsible for her happiness; if not there was hell to pay. Because of her, I would pick violent fights and accuse you of anything she could think of. I would call you every foul name too. When we were together, we were so broken. We would be angry at anyone trying to leave us. We once were angry at one of my girlfriends who planned an outing with her friend and never invited me. The sparks flew! I was so angry that I punched a window and broke it. Furious, I left the house to search for her. She knew I'd go crazy when she left, but it was okay, because that's how we loved each other. I came home and found her sleeping in the car, waiting for me. Little Tamika never wanted to be alone, so she created rules that I would try to force upon others. You were not allowed to live without her and when you wanted to be alone, she would throw temper tantrums – full of anger, control, and manipulation. I didn't know it at the time, but Little Tamika controlled my life. She took me down a path of self destruction and I became a terror to myself and others.

I was naïve about functional relationships. It seemed like I always ended up with women who would lie and cheat. It's important that you always ask questions if you ever decide to be sexually active. Ask them if they have anything that you need to know about before you're intimate with each of them. One of my female partners gave me an STD and then lied about it. I blame myself because I didn't ask her questions about her sexual health. When I found out about my STD, I did ask, and I was lied to repeatedly as my body reacted to the disease. I wasn't with anyone else at the time, so I knew it was her. She continually lied about it while I suffered. One night, things got out of control, the cops were called, and then, she left me. It was a double whammy; hurt because she lied and because she left. The reason I'm being so transparent is because I want to stress the importance of asking people if they have any diseases you need to know about. I didn't realize that I was still carrying these feelings until I was reading the final touches of this book. If you are intentionally hurting people by not telling them the truth because of your own pain, that is between you and God.

Please, learn from me. Don't stay with someone who won't give you the freedom to choose to protect your sexual health. If you end up like me, you'll be angry and take it out on yourself and that person. Never look at their faces and body, just because they look good on the outside, doesn't mean that there isn't something going on within their body – be responsible for yourself. Know your worth! You don't have to live in fear if you do get an STD. You're still a worthy person. I felt the same way, but back then I didn't know my worth and was depressed. Having a disease made me feel guilty, shameful, and dirty.

Another thing that made me feel shameful was an experience I had a nightclub. One night I was partying with one of my girlfriends. We were outside at the back of the club talking and happen to see the cops roll by. Suddenly, they put the car in reverse, got out of the vehicle and walked towards us. I was already intoxicated and had a habit of always having my hands in my pockets. Two white males approached us and asked us what we were doing. I stated that we were just talking. One cop told me to take my hands out of my pockets. Thinking he just wanted to make sure there was nothing in my pockets, I took my hands out of my pockets and then showed him that there was nothing in my pockets. I put my hands back in my pockets – remember I was intoxicated and really wasn't thinking clearly. The cop told me again, "I said, take your hands out of your pockets!" The next thing I knew, he grabbed me by the hand and threw me into a brick wall. He assaulted me. I ended up with a black and blue bruise on my buttocks and a cut on my hand. I had asked the cop for his badge number, but he gave me the number of a black cop that no longer worked in the department. I tried to report the incident, but without the correct badge number, I couldn't go any further. I was black and gay and because of that, I was assaulted. No one deserves to be disrespected. Whether straight or gay, stay alert at all times.

I needed someone to talk to about the issues I was experiencing, but the older women that I had looked up to really weren't model citizens. They were just as bad as I was. I needed something to help ease the pain and I became curious about loving things that were considered by most as bad. My addiction took off from there and it wasn't too long before I dabbled in drugs and fell in love with them too.

When you first take drugs, they give you the illusion of being happy, joyous, and free. Well, that is until you pissed me off, then it wasn't good for you or me.

It's nothing like being stuck on a drug that makes you eat like crazy just because you inhaled it like a cigarette. Smoking made me feel like I was in control and that I could conquer the world. I believed that the drugs were taking good care of me, but instead I was just dependent on them. It put me inside a bubble, a temporary shield from reality, and I walked around in a make-believe world. In my world, I could be anyone I wanted to be. Pretending became my everyday way of life because as long as I was high, the pain was bearable. The only issue was that I still needed someone by my side. The drugs took care of the thorn, but my search continued for someone to help me pretend that my life was great. I believed that I needed someone in my make-believe world to complete my life. It was really Little Tamika crying out again. I had to satisfy her and feed her, or she would burst my bubble. What made it so ironic was that she cried out for intimacy, yet when I was in a relationship, she would sabotage it. I could never have a healthy, functional relationship with anyone. I could never last more than a moment in happiness, unless it was during sex. I wanted love, but only found lust. I found myself in multiple relationships, mostly as the third person though. A lot of women were attracted to me as a third wheel. I was only there to make their female partners jealous when they were having problems. I could never be in a one on one, exclusive relationship. None of the women ever left their partner. I was caught up in the game of trying to prove my worth and be someone that I really wasn't. I was just an insecure, little girl in men's clothes. All Little Tamika was doing was playing dress up because she looked like the man that left her. Somehow, that meant that she looked better as a man. So, I continued to venture into the lesbian lifestyle.

No matter the relationship, I told myself that the person was in my life to help me get over all of my issues. The ups and downs didn't alarm me. I thought I was finally getting the love that I deserved. I thought it was going to fix me. I thought I was lost at a young age, but when I tasted the forbidden fruit of lesbianism, I fell so deep into a sunken place that my mind was overcome with deception. Today, I look back and see that I saw life from a depraved mindset. In reality, it was trouble for me and whomever decided to get mixed up with my wounded soul.

The vicious circle that I lived in was my own self-made prison. I felt like I couldn't find my way out and it was only getting worse. I realized I was never happy and that my need to find someone to fix me was destroying me. I was slowly accepting the unacceptable in my life because of my wounds. I had never addressed those issues before. I couldn't handle the truth, but now I was forced to see that I was dying on the inside. I always appeared to be strong and confident, but eventually, my wounds were exposed. As I became more and more aware of my flaws, I began to gain weight. I tried to fix it with a diet, but I could never finish it. Self-hatred begot sabotage and it started a downhill journey of even more self destruction.

If you saw me from day to day, I appeared happy, but on the inside, I was living in fear of rejection. I was full of insecurity and anger. My broken pieces were so evident that the people closest to me couldn't handle the half of a person that I was, but my denial made me think that I was okay. As Little Tamika kept me bound, she also sought to take hostages in every relationship, and you could tell how the "hostage-ship" would end. I realized relationships weren't working out for me. I could tell that I was going against the grain, but I still tried to fix, manage, and control the outcome. I was the last one in the relationship to find out that we were emotionally over. It was easy to let go sexually, but Little Tamika would cry out until the bitter end. The outcome was always pain and it left me in a fetal position for a very long time.

Chapter 4
WILLING TO SEEK GREATER

I was growing tired of the fight, but I kept fighting. Eventually someone saw that I was in need of help. They urged me to stop doing drugs and so, I went to rehab, but I didn't go to get clean. I had heard about Narcotics Anonymous and I stepped into my first meeting and told them I needed help. I was only going to keep the girl because if I stayed clean, daddy wouldn't leave me like before. The relationship didn't last, but I surrendered to the program and established a commitment to stay clean with the help of God, a sponsor, attending meetings, and their step work to get to the root of my issues. I stopped using mood and mind-altering chemicals and things were beginning to make sense. I also stayed away from the clubs since they were my other choice drug. It was a challenge to live without being high because I could no longer live in a fantasy, make-believe world, but I continued to stay clean and embarked on a journey of internal healing.

The recovery process dealt with step work. Through step work, you'd find the underlying issues of your drug abuse. Step one was all about whatever brought you into the recovery process. I found out what made me want to stay high and learned how it was just an illusion. The recovery process says, "everything must change". Initially, you don't know how to live with or without the drug, so they send you a mentor that guides you through it. They understood me and how I thought. That made the process easier. When I got to the 11th step there was conflict. My Christian lifestyle didn't match. The problem was that recovery was never ending. You're always going to meetings trying to find yourself, but I was grateful for the recovery process because I was shown how to live in the moment.

Through all of this, I still wanted love and so I was still a lesbian seeking a relationship to make me happy. However, you will always attract who you are within. I didn't know how to love, so all I could do was love you based on the conditions of our relationship. When it was good, I was good. When things were bad, they were really bad. I thought that once I stopped getting high, all of my problems would get better. I thought I'd have better relationships and I'd finally be happy. Instead, it seemed as if all my issues came to the surface. There they were, in my face and it didn't feel good. I tried X, Y, and Z to fill the wounds and pains that had resurfaced. I no longer had the drugs to make me believe that everything was okay. The thoughts from my past began to haunt me. Thoughts of being abandoned, rejected, and unworthy all came rushing into my mind and I was afraid. I was beginning to think that I was going crazy and I wanted to get high to make it stop. I think this is where most people relapse, however, there was something that kept me from going back to drugs. I later realized that something was my spirit connecting with God. He was calling me, and I didn't know it.

I continued my recovery process, but Little Tamika was exhausting to live with. She kept me living in fear, led me to false happiness, and pressed me to search for many unfulfilling things. She was the vehicle that the spirit of abandonment needed to completely drain me. It was a gloomy way of life and

I was blinded by pain. She wanted to feed my inner demons, but I couldn't find anything that would satisfy them, even while in recovery. One day I realized that they couldn't be satisfied; it was impossible to feed them. What I needed was a real internal healing. It was an inside job, and I could hear something on the inside telling me, "Just believe in me daughter."

It was ironic that a lady from my job who had been a wild friend of mine had just started to get her life together too. Her name was Angela (I call her Mother Angie today). She started going to church and would begin to tell me about God. I didn't want to be disrespectful, but I really didn't want to hear what she had to say. She would tell me that God put it on her heart to let me know that I should read the Bible, specifically, the book of Leviticus. I never understood it, but I really didn't want to anyway. Back then I didn't know God. I didn't know He could fill my voids with joy, something that would give me the strength to overcome and block those spirits, even at an early age. I didn't know because I didn't have a background or foundation in church. My only connection to God was when my Grandmother prayed the 23rd Psalm every night before bed. When my father left me, the spirit of abandonment and its friends told me that God didn't love me, and I really believed them. When my father left, I truly thought it was all my fault.

Later on, I decided to try God. I am not saying that it is easy, but I finally became willing to seek something that would no longer damage my spirit. It takes a certain level of surrender and you really have to be gentle with yourself throughout the journey. The recovery process helped me in the moment, but I needed more. I had to be saved to begin the process with God and believe that Jesus died to erase all my sins. Being saved means I asked Jesus Christ to be part of my life because I believed in Him and His power to cleanse my sins. I believed that He died to cleanse my sins, but God raised Him from the dead. Finally, I said it out loud, I confessed that I believed. I was saved many times, but always went back to my lifestyle. However, one particular time that I was saved, I knew that it was time to turn my will over to God.

Chapter 5
A NEW BEGINNING

Even though I was saved, my walk with Jesus Christ was not a stable one because I still wanted to do what I wanted to do. It was shaky because I didn't want to leave where I came from. I had a hunger for God that I truly didn't understand. I knew the lesbian lifestyle wasn't for me anymore, but I didn't want to let it go. At first, I didn't fully believe that I could change, so life was a daily struggle. However, as time went on, I knew that if I totally submitted to God, my life would really change and that scared me. The thought of leaving behind what I had known for so long was terrifying, so I didn't seek God's face wholeheartedly.

I would still cry to God to take away the pain, and He would pull on me to give up the lifestyle that was causing me the most pain. Eventually, He won. God began to turn everything upside down. The process of changing from the inside out was extremely frightening. I began to have bouts of depression all over again, and something new; I was dealing with suicide. I was wearing some of my pain as weight gain and even weight loss. The vicious cycle of unworthiness, unforgiveness, and abuse had contributed to this. I wanted to get high to get away from these feelings, but I didn't. I'm grateful for that. The changes that were occurring just seemed as if God was digging up my past and making me face it. I felt the voids, pains, and disappointments resurface, but this time I had God with me. I could no longer ease them with the pleasure of women or drugs. Instead, I allowed Christ to fill the voids and in doing so, I felt the chains of my past began breaking. Although I was still scared, I knew that where I came from was killing me from within and I no longer wanted any part of it. I was serious about changing, so I connected with a church and fully submitted to God.

My beginning journey with Christ was a long process, but I was able to withstand the *"wiles of the devil"* (Ephesians 6:11) one day at a time. I began to surrender my life over to God on a daily basis. Some days it was minute by minute, but when my abandonment began to surface, the only thing that eased it was prayer. I began to see how God was talking to me through people. I didn't like it and I tried to ignore the signs. I had several people tell me God wanted me to leave the gay lifestyle. One family member would tell me that God's hand was on my shoulder. Finally, I submitted to the fact that I had to let go of women to complete this process and start the next. I thought it would be easy, but it really wasn't. My tomboy lesbianism lifestyle was the mask that covered the pain of being abandoned, rejected, and abused at a young age. My tough persona was hiding the trauma, but just as you peel an onion, Jesus peeled away all that I ever knew. He revealed it and then He cleansed the wounds. He eased the pain and helped me deal with my troubles. As I started reading God's Word, I became a true believer of His Word.

The hardest thing I went through was detaching myself from people who would hinder my new beginning. I wanted to be accepted, but I was being judged. I started to withdraw from people and stay around those that made me feel safe, but it wasn't many. Little Tamika was crying out with fear, but I turned to Jesus and I had better days than I ever had in my past. It was surreal to see the same group of people that public cry out against judgement on their sexual preference turn on me when I decided to leave their group. I was changing and the other lesbians were judging me. I felt like an outcast. I remember people saying, "Oh, you're not gay anymore?" I overheard people talking about me. They'd say things like, "I hear Tamika is with men now." My response to them was always, "No, I'm with God now and there are some things that I will no longer do." The sad part about it was that the people that were talking about me were struggling with their own mess.

You would think that I could find peace inside a church, but the church judged me too. The older women would stare at my shoes. At the time, I was still dressing in men's clothing, so my shoes weren't feminine at all. It made me feel uncomfortable, but I didn't care because I knew God placed me there for a reason. No one there could get rid of me and I wasn't uncomfortable enough that I wanted to leave. The only reason I would leave was if someone touched a nerve or issue of mine that I wasn't ready to deal with or even desired to be healed from.

I was living in two different worlds, the recovery world and the church world. In the recovery world you are able to find the God of your own understanding. This means that you can't say anything related to religion. Muslims can't thank Allah and Christians can't thank Jesus. You could only say something about a "higher power", something that was loving, caring, and greater than yourself. This kept the recovery belief system nonjudgmental. In the church world, you believed in Jesus Christ. It was beginning to make a lot of sense to me, but I didn't know how to balance the two worlds. It made me feel anxious, and I knew I would soon have to choose one or the other. I slowly began to choose church, but it didn't fit into my gay lifestyle. The next best thing to do was to try a gay church. I attended a gay church, but I didn't fit. I had to ask God what to do because I was confused. I told him, 'God, I don't fit in with the gays and I don't fit in with the straights, so where do I belong?' God stated to me that I belonged to Him and that homosexuality isn't what He wanted for me. I surrendered because I knew that God was deeply healing me, and He wanted me to trust him.

It was hard for me to trust anyone, but I tried because I could tell I was on a new level. How? I was beginning to love myself! That made me believe in the possibility that all things are working out for my good (Romans 8:28). I couldn't continue to believe in my out of date belief system any longer; it was killing me from within. God stated that he would never leave me nor forsake me (Hebrews 13:5), so why fear? He has not given us a spirit of fear (II Timothy 1:7) so why should I walk in it? Logically, I knew that I shouldn't and didn't need to, but sometimes I did. I'm grateful that God kept speaking even when He knew I was afraid and would try to walk backwards. When I became more and more disobedient, I had to face more and more fears. They were fears concerning the mandate on my life. I knew that God was eventually going to send me to find and bring out others that were in the homosexual lifestyle. I had to accept the fact that God would use me to lead others out of the cave of abandonment, abuse, and many other sins. However, every time I would run away from who I was meant to be, I would come back stronger. Well, first I had to repent of all my unrighteousness. I had to do this because no one can be on God's side and continue to do sinful things. God hates sin, but He still loves the sinner. Things just don't work like that in God's world. It can be hard to stay righteous, but when you have a lifestyle of fasting and prayer and a good covering or a good Pastor, then it doesn't seem that hard.

There were men and women praying for me. They were people who were on God's side and knew that the enemy, the devil, was mad that I had chosen to give up living a homosexual lifestyle. I could tell he was very angry with me because I could feel strong attacks in my mind. They seemed to come from every possible angle, but prayer and perseverance were the keys to overcoming them. Prayer was an important part of my life because it seemed as if depression was my best friend for a long time. I was also fighting many inner demons, you know, the ones from my childhood. It was such an internal struggle that I didn't know whether I was coming or going. So many thoughts fought to take over my mind – guilt, shame, rejection, and more. Because of this struggle, I finally left the world of recovery. It felt as if they didn't understand me anymore. I didn't know what I was going through, so I made the decision to leave. It's hard to stay around people that don't understand what you're going through. It's hard for people to help you when they have no clue about what's going on internally, and it was difficult to explain to people that didn't believe in my God. To this day I struggle to reconnect with them. How could I explain that I was consumed with guilt and shame for living an unholy and depraved lifestyle for more than twenty years? Would they even understand why I considered it unholy and depraved? Could they possibly identify with my feelings? I knew I lived a sick life while in homosexuality, and I cringed that I had to start life all over again. I wasn't a young girl anymore. These thoughts clouded my mind and encouraged me to keep making excuses. However, there's one thing I learned – excuses keep you stuck in a destructive pattern. This was especially true since God had cleaned me up and taken me out of a painful lifestyle. I came to terms with that and remembered that I didn't need to look back at my past mistakes, I needed to look forward – toward my new future with Christ.

Chapter 6
THE TRANSFORMATION

As I continued on my journey with Christ, I was urged to try another church, one that would be more accepting of me, despite my clothing. I was still wearing men clothes as God was working on the inside of me. I didn't allow the judgement of others to affect me. I was already feeling insecure, so what they thought didn't matter anymore. I knew that God was creating in me a clean heart and renewing in me a right spirit (Psalm 51:10) and I had to continue even when I was weary and faint hearted. I felt like I was living in two different worlds as I walked through this life changing process.

An older woman at my church named Mother Burnside urged me to attend a women's service. She attended the service once a month on a Tuesday night. It was a service for women that wanted more from God and didn't care whether they were from different denominations. All they cared about was worshipping Jesus and allowing Him to heal them of their pain. After service they had refreshments where we would network and fellowship with each other. I remember one service I attended, it was a Cancer Deliverance service for women who had battled cancer or was still battling it. The preacher was Pastor Robbin Hargrove (she's now an Apostle), and she called everyone up to the altar that night and began to pray. As she was praying, she called me over to her. I was still dressed in men's attire, but she called me up closer and began to tell me what God was saying to her. She told me that God wanted to give me a crown of glory. As she explained what God said to her, another preacher picked up a silver tiara and placed it on my head. Imagine how I felt being dressed as a stud (man) as these church folks wanted me to wear a tiara. I was saying to myself, "Really God?" I was so upset and embarrassed by what was happening. All I wanted to do was crawl under something and curl into a ball after they crowned me. I was afraid to take it off in front of the people, so I just walked around in fear and in anger until the end of the service. I wasn't angry because they called me out while I was a lesbian, I was angry because I felt unworthy. It was eating me alive!

My instructions were to go home and look at myself in the mirror with the tiara. I did it reluctantly. I struggled with the thought that I would enjoy it. No one knows that I went home and really tried to look in the mirror to see my beauty or even God's beauty and at first, I couldn't see it. I would ask God, "Why?" He would respond, "Why not? You are my daughter. You deserve to be crowned daughter. You are not by yourself and I am in need of thee." I would peek at myself and think about it, then a wave of discouragement would hit me, and I'd pull it off. I thought me being a feminine woman was impossible. Despite my feelings, I would continue wearing it. However, I cried because the identity that I had known for so long was slowly fading away with the help of God and the women that He put in my life.

Later, I decided to try Apostle Robbin's church and I ended up joining. I worshipped there because I could feel God's spirit during service. When I felt God's spirit rest on me, all I could do was cry. That's all I can still do! I cried like a baby and I had a tingling sensation that made me feel like I was loved by God.

It was a great feeling because I knew nothing else mattered if He loved me. One day, I felt the need to change my appearance. Unfortunately, I don't remember how it all happened, but when I came back to church, I told Apostle Robbin. I explained that I was ready to let go of my grave clothes. The term "grave clothes" refers to the Bible story about Lazarus, a man who was dead for four days, but was raised to life by Jesus (John 11:1-44). Once he came out of the grave, he was still bound by the grave clothes that people had wrapped him in. He needed someone to help him take them off. When I approached my Pastor with my thoughts, a couple ladies were there with her. They responded to me saying, "You don't even know how to shop for women's things." They determined that I needed help. Then Apostle Robbin said, "Let's make it happen, it would be fun!" Her mother, Pastor Peaches, overheard us and sprang into action also. We planned a date and went shopping.

I thought I was fat and ugly, and those feelings would arise inside of me that day. Dressing as a man was normal to me, so I was uncomfortable walking into the female clothing section. I knew God was changing me as layers were falling off of me. I wanted to change, but just didn't know how. Truth be told, I was surprised that Pastor Peaches supported me by giving me three hundred dollars. I went to the store with Apostle Robbin, Ambassador Rhonda, Deacon Brenda, and Mother Carson. They pulled clothes off the racks and put them into my hand so I could play dress up in the dressing room. Despite always being insecure of the way I dressed, I was so uncomfortable of this change, but I wasn't alone and that helped me. Apostle Robbin told me that a girl always needs a pair of black pumps. I am still learning to walk in those pumps today – LOL! Ambassador Rhonda had me try on a form fitting shirt and I said, "Really, Rhonda? Really?" I can laugh now, but it wasn't so cute and funny as I was in transition. Even though I didn't say anything at that point, other than thank you, each of those ladies made a huge impact in my life during my Cinderella transition. God was changing everything that I knew, and He used those women to help me. As they helped me remove my grave clothes, God was removing everything that the grave clothes meant. The men's clothing represented a lesbian lifestyle, abuse, and abandonment. Again, as I dressed in women's clothing, I was forced to deal with each of them. God was digging deeper and deeper inside of me. He was getting to the root of my issues. At first, I was afraid, but I knew God was with me.

I will always remember the time I went back to dressing in baggy clothing and Ambassador Rhonda said, "Now you know God has taken you out of the grave clothes, so don't go back!" She didn't say it in a mean or embarrassing tone, it was out of love and I respected her in hindsight. I dressed as a woman while in church and that was easy, but when I went home, I was still dressing as a man. I continued to read and meditate on God's word. The frustration of struggling between my new clothes and my grave clothes was getting to me. I began coping with it by eating. When I exercised, you wouldn't be able to tell I gained weight, but when I didn't work out, it was evident. I had a hard time dealing with my weight gain and it showed in my attitude. I am still receiving healing in this area. I know I'm being healed because God brought it to my attention, and I am finally talking about it. The real issue with my weight came from me feeling ashamed to wear women's clothing. I felt ashamed because I was changing again, and it was easier to blame people, places, and things for my issues. No matter what, I kept moving forward with God's plan. It was almost as if a still, small voice was speaking in my ear saying, "Keep going, I am with you daughter." I did and as the surgery of my spirit continued, things seemed to be better.

I can never say that I didn't receive love from The Embassy. God used each and every one of these women, and more, to help me on my journey of identity deception to deliverance from a false self-identity. I am grateful to the women's group that crowned me, the Women of Deliverance (WOD) Spiritual Midwives. I am especially grateful to Mother Burnside who took me to my first WOD service. God truly used her to plant a seed. I love them all so much.

Chapter 7
HE'S CALLING YOU

I love talking about God and how he changed my life. He took away the pain and restored my soul. I knew that he had a purpose for my life, but I had to be obedient to the call. I feel blessed to have transformed from one lifestyle to a Godly lifestyle. Can you stand to be blessed by God? If your answer is yes, then there are some things you must do. It isn't hard, but it requires a strict obedience. The change in my life was due to my commitment despite my inability to see where God was taking me. It took a great level of loyalty on my part, something I have never given to anyone before, however, it was the most rewarding thing I've ever done. I have been touched by Jesus Christ and I will never be the same again. God sanctified me, but it was a real wilderness experience. A wilderness experience means that I felt alone throughout the process. I loved being validated by other people, so God had to strip that away, so that I knew it was important to be validated by Him alone. I felt lost, but I really wasn't. He was molding me into someone different and it was just the beginning.

God wants all of our attention and wants to be connected to us, but there are things we have done that has disconnected us from Him. God will get your attention, whether gently or hardcore. However, the more that you seek His face, the more He will reveal Himself to you. He will also reveal His will or His plan for your life. Whenever you get fearful, just do what I did. I read His scriptures and it uplifted me when I trusted in it.

I know there are people in the gay lifestyle that want to come out if it, but don't know that it is possible to not only come out but stay out. I'm a witness that it is possible, but you have to connect to people that have the same mindset. You cannot hang out with other lesbians or other gays and think that you can change. If you do so, you will eventually believe that it is okay and will return to your old ways. The key is to seek Him and search for Him because you will find

Him. I had a hunger to find Him – one that I never had for anyone else. Here's my advice. When you are on a spiritual healing journey, never get involved with anyone intimately in the beginning of the process. Dust yourself off and start taking baby steps towards God, just as I did. Ezekiel 16:6 in the New King James states,

"And when I passed by you
and saw you struggling in your own blood,
I said to you in your blood,
"Live"! Yes, I said to you in your blood, "Live!"

This scripture really stands out for me because I was living with my own wounds and afflictions. Although I thought I was okay, I really wasn't. Take a minute and think about your own issues that keep you in darkness or "struggling in your own blood". What did you use to fill the void? How did you feel when you were chasing that person, place, or thing? What's your outcome? Can you stop chasing without God in the picture? Do your euphoric feelings last long without God in the picture? If not, then you should seek His face and develop a relationship with Him.

The truth is you will never stop searching for God, even after you find Him. There's so much to Him, so many levels, and with every level, you will experience change. Even as I write, I continue to seek His face. I know that I could never feel this way with anyone else, and all it took was a consistent, serious relationship with Him. I no longer believe in false love and I'm no longer ashamed to tell my story. If you believe that God has touched your heart as you read this book, contact me and let's fellowship about the goodness of the Lord.

Chapter 8
HOW TO ANSWER THE CALL

If you feel that God is calling you all you have to do is answer the call. Sometimes the simplest things can seem so hard. I want to share with you how I answered the call by submitting to God, praying, and reading the Bible.

How to Submit to God

I would cry to God and ask Him what was wrong with me. I didn't hear anything in the beginning because I was unable to hear. Submitting to God is a process that would be easy if you would just trust Him. That was not my story. I distrusted, doubted, and didn't believe, and it made everything difficult.

Submitting to God as a new creation in Christ is a daily walk of repentance from unrighteousness It's also developing a relationship. When I was baptized, before I was submerged in the water, I repented of my sins. I came up a new creation of Christ. I had to learn through my mistakes that God is in control of all things. As I walked with God, I knew that my life was changing even if it wasn't evident on the outside. I began to believe in the intangible evidence that was building inside as long as I sought his face daily. The more I submitted to Him, the more I wanted to be like Him. I prayed continually, and in prayer He would reveal things to me, and it strengthened me to lay down sins that were killing me daily. I never thought that it would change my gay lifestyle, but in the end, I was open, and I lost the appetite for women. I was shocked! Being a lesbian was all that I knew, and it was being taken from me. I was afraid, but God didn't give me a spirit of fear (II Timothy 1:7). I kept pressing and moving forward by staying in the Word. I couldn't hang around any women that were still living that lifestyle. It was lonely at first, but prayer and Godly fellowship was key in my life, so I kept pressing and it really became a lot easier. I prayed in my heavenly language and that gave me strength.

The people needed to push you to the next level will be sent to you by God. Just be patient and trust Him. God became my lover and He guided me every day. He will not force anyone to change. I made the decision to be open to Him and change. He let me know that how I was living was no longer conducive to my spirit. I wanted to please God, so I read the Word and it became life to me. Being gay was no longer an option. It was a sin, and I didn't want to practice it anymore. If you feel like I felt, read the first chapter of the book of Romans. It will help you on your journey.

How to Pray

Prayer is something that is very important in any believer's life. I learned how to pray when I was going through another tough time in my life. My mom was diagnosed with Cancer and I prayed for her and with her. I would always read Psalm 23 and then began praying that my mom wouldn't suffer anymore. I really didn't get into the Word like I should have.

Prayer takes practice and building a relationship with God takes patience. I didn't really go deeper with

God until my mom passed away. I suffered from depression when she left. I thank God for my recovery and for the people who supported me. My life took another turn when I lost my job. I learned to pray by using the scriptures that I was learning. I also fasted when I prayed. I would lay prostrate which means I laid down facing the floor. I put my arms out to the side. In a way, it's the same pose that Jesus was crucified in, except I was on the ground on my stomach. This was a habit of mine to go deeper in God.

Another part of prayer is praying in your heavenly language as stated in Acts 2, verses one through four. One day, I had gone up to the ocean, a place I've loved going to ever since my baptism, and I cried out to God about a woman. That day, I began to speak in tongues! I was so excited because I previously prayed for my heavenly language. I desired this language because it's how Christians directly communicate with God. No one else understands unless God gives them revelation. At first, it seemed like I was saying the same thing over and over, but as you grow in God, the language changes. You will develop and cultivate boldness, authority, and power. These gifts were given to Believers after the resurrection of Jesus Christ and the infilling of the Holy Ghost (Acts 2:1-21).

As I continued to grow in Christ, God had me meet a prayer warrior. Her name is Overseer Daniels and she taught me to pray for long periods of time in my prayer language. It was challenging at first, but the more you pray in your heavenly language, the stronger you become in Christ. You will grow in Christ as you pray and read the Word of God, which is also called, the 'Sword of the Spirit' (Ephesians 6:17).

How to Read the Bible

As a new believer, many people told me to read the Gospels (Matthew, Mark, Luke and John). These books detail the life of Jesus Christ. As I grew in Him and developed a hunger to read the Word, I found that it fed me daily. I would ask God during my prayer time, what He would have me to read and meditate on for the day. It was always something that I needed. If there is anything that you do not understand, there are people on the same journey that will help you. There are mentors for one on one sessions. At the Embassy, I am learning that I am always in training as an Ambassador for Christ. I know that I must put on the whole armor of God each and every day (Ephesians 6:10-20) because I am always in combat for the Lord against an enemy who wants to deceive the world. I must always walk in the spirit and have the fruit of the Spirit (Galatians 5:16-26). You must always remember that the devil is here in this world to kill, steal, and destroy, but God comes so that we may have life, and have it more abundantly (John 10:10). Reading the Bible will give you new revelation and wisdom the more you read it. Don't be afraid to ask God questions because it will be provided to you.

Giving Your Life to Christ

Do you believe that Jesus died for your sins? If so, the Bible tells us: "that if you confess with your mouth the Lord Jesus and believe in your heart that God has raised Him from the dead, you will be saved" (Romans 10:9).

If you believe that God is seeking you to come into the kingdom of God, then please pray with me. Speak the following words out loud:

Jesus I am a sinner and I ask for your forgiveness. I want a change in my life, and I can't do it by myself. I have tried and I get worse trying to change myself. I repent of all unrighteousness. "Create in me a clean heart, O God; and renew a right spirit within me" (Psalms 51:10). I believe in my heart that God raised Jesus from the dead and that Jesus died with all power and rose again on the third day. I believe God is washing me with the blood of Jesus. Thank you, Jesus that your blood is applied to my life to cancel the spiritual death sentence and will make me a new from the inside out. From this day forward, I make Jesus my Lord and Savior.

As you grow in Jesus by studying the word, praying in the spirit and fasting, you will be strengthened every day. Give yourself a break and allow Jesus to guide you. It may not be easy. Look at His life and what He did for us sinners. He was without sin and took all of our nasty sins and nailed it to the cross. The blood of Jesus is renewing us every day if we allow it. Take a leap of faith and bask in the Glory of our heavenly Father because you are now a new creation in Christ Jesus as this scripture states: "Therefore, if anyone is in Christ, he is a new creation; old things have passed away; behold, all things have become new" (II Corinthians 5:17).

ABOUT THE AUTHOR

Tamika Strickland began her walk with God when He used her as a prayer warrior for her mother as she faced breast cancer. As Tamika prayed, she realized that she had a connection with Christ Jesus. Tamika didn't go any further at that time even after God cleaned her up from drugs and alcohol on Sept. 16, 2000 (Praise God!). God called her mother home on Oct. 30, 2003, and she was glad to have a foundation in recovery as a mentor for men and women like herself before her mother passed away. Tamika loved helping others as well as helping herself.

Tamika didn't grow up in church, so when she finally walked into church, she cried all through service. *"She sought the Lord and He heard her cry."* She began to seek a relationship with Jesus Christ, walked into **The Embassy** and found a safety net when becoming a partner under the teachings of Apostle Robbin Hargrove. Tamika began her service in the house of God on the Praise and Worship Team and was very humbled to sing for the Lord. Since 2011, she wanted to be a part of the ministry called **Women of Deliverance (WOD)** but didn't join until 2013, ultimately graduating in 2014 (Class #5).

Tamika knows that God is *real* and has done a miraculous surgery of the spirit in her. She has taken off the grave clothes that held her BOUND, and walks with self-love, self-worth, and self-respect. In September 2014, God has elevated her as a Teacher for our fivefold ministry at **The Embassy**. She also has responded to the call to attend **Last Day Remnant Bible College** to deepen her relationship with Christ in September 2014. Tamika is blessed to be taught in both ministries by Senior Pastor Apostle Robbin and Pastor Earl Hargrove. She is currently training as an Evangelist-Elect.

Her favorite scripture is II Timothy 1:7:

'For God hath not given us a spirit of fear; but of power, and of love, and a sound mind.'